Cora the Little Crab

by Becca Heddle

illustrated by Craig Shuttlewood

OXFORD
UNIVERSITY PRESS

Cora was a little crab.
She ran on the sand.

"Come back," said her sister, Oona. "You can not run left to right."

"You must run like that gull.
It is how animals run," said Oona.

Cora sank down.

"Are you sure?" said Cora.

"Look at that dog," said Oona.
"It runs like the gull, too."

The dog ran near them.
It was rushing after a ball.

Cora had a go.
Her feet took her off to the left.

Then they took her off to the right.

"It is too hard," said Cora.
"Can you show me?"

Big sister Oona had a go.
She went left to right, too!

Just then, some crabs ran past.

They all run like us, Oona!

We will run like crabs now.

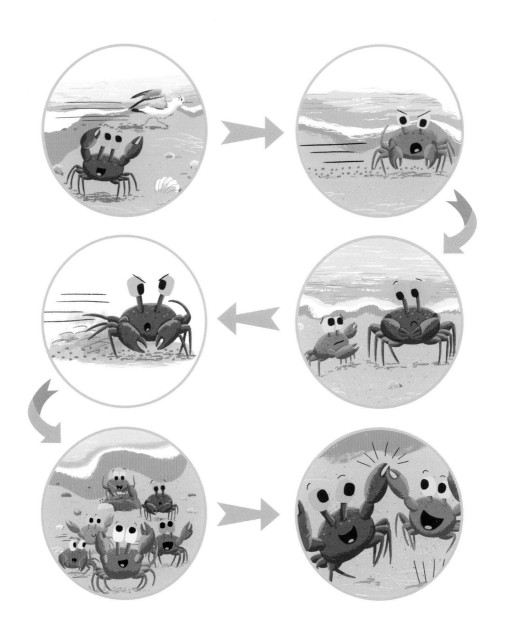

 Encourage the child to use the pictures to retell the story.